You know the old story of the chameleon.
Put him on green, he turns green.
Put him on black, he turns black.
But if you put him on plaid he explodes.

—Jean Seberg

DENNIS ADAMS
Double Feature

Published in conjunction with the exhibition: Double Feature
March 27th – April 26th, Kent Gallery, NY

92 pages, 40 black and white plates

Publication no. 38

541 West 25th Street, New York, NY 10001
www.kentgallery.com

Editor: Jeanne Marie Wasilik
Image editing: Paul Colin/Cezanne Studio, NY
Book design: Dennis Adams, Paul Colin, Daniel Dror

ISBN: 978-1-878607-77-5

First Edition: 2000 copies

Permanent Printing Limited, China

DENNIS ADAMS

DOUBLE FEATURE

KENT

Dennis Adams's *Double Feature* is a series of composite "stills" collaged from individual frames grabbed from Jean-Luc Godard's *Breathless* (1959) and Gillo Pontecorvo's *The Battle of Algiers* (1965). In these constructed images Jean Seberg, the co-star of *Breathless*, has been displaced from her celebrated stroll along the Champs-Élysées in Paris, where she hawked the *New York Herald Tribune* with Jean-Paul Belmondo at her side, and relocated in Algiers during Algeria's struggle for independence from French rule, where she walks the city's war-torn streets.

The streets are those depicted in *The Battle of Algiers*. Seberg's cropped hair and her *Herald Tribune* T-shirt, along with the newspapers and little white handbag she carries, mark her iconic identity as she walks out of *Breathless* and into the demonstrations, checkpoints, and skirmishes of the Algerian Revolution. Her scene as news vendor, which was for Godard little more than a device to establish her American identity and to set up the flirtation with Belmondo, is recontextualized as an index to the unfolding historical events we find her passing through. Seberg is recast as an allegorical figure walking the fault line between the roles of messenger bearing the news and frontline witness to its making.

Seberg's role in *Breathless* will always be identified with the *New York Herald Tribune*, the famed English-language paper produced and distributed in Paris, later renamed the *International Herald Tribune*. The T-shirt with the newspaper's logo that Seberg wore as she strolled down the Champs-Élysées was a common sight in Paris during the 1950s and 60s, when it was worn by the young English-speaking women the *Herald Tribune* employed to sell papers on the streets.

While both *Breathless* and *The Battle of Algiers* depict the same historical window of time, and even share some of the era's cinema verité, handheld camera aesthetic, they could not be more incompatible in their narrative pacing and political stance. Seberg and Belmondo wander aimlessly through Paris, attentive only to their tenuous relationship and the momentary circumstances of their lives, while the cast of characters in Algiers, on both sides of the conflict, tests the absolute limits of violence in a battle to defend opposing ideals.

Released in 1966 and initially banned in France, *The Battle of Algiers* commemorates the Algerian uprising against French colonial rule, a struggle that lasted from 1954 to 1962. Considered one of the most influential films in the history of political cinema, it revolutionized the genre with its quasi-documentary style and use of former insurgents to reenact historical events. While Pontecorvo is clearly sympathetic to the Algerians' struggle, he rejects the bare-knuckle propaganda style of Soviet masters Vsevolod Pudovkin and Sergei Eisenstein in favor of a more even handed depiction of both sides of the conflict. This has the effect of amplifying the viewers' ethical tension and also points to why the film has become a global cinematic primer for both insurgents and state police. Since its release, liberation groups have viewed *The Battle of Algiers* as a manifesto of revolutionary strategy, including the Black Panthers and the IRA, both of whom adapted its techniques in their training manuals. After September 11 the film became essential viewing for both jihadists and US government and military personnel. Its depictions of resistance through violent guerilla tactics, as well as of state-sponsored torture has proved to be prophetic in the context of the current conflicts in Iraq and Afghanistan.

Released in 1960, *Breathless* is Godard's first full-length feature and a manifesto of New Wave cinema. The story is set in Paris and revolves around the relationship between a petty gangster, played by Belmondo, and an American student, played by Seberg. Referencing Hollywood genres at every turn, Godard throws his young stars into a fast-forward relationship spliced together by an unpredictable collage of aggressive jump-cuts and nonchalant super-long takes. Conventions of narrative cinema take a back seat as the film unleashes a radical new aesthetic joined at the hip to the portrayal of an unprecedented youthful recklessness.

DOUBLE FEATURE

a call to prayer or a call to arms

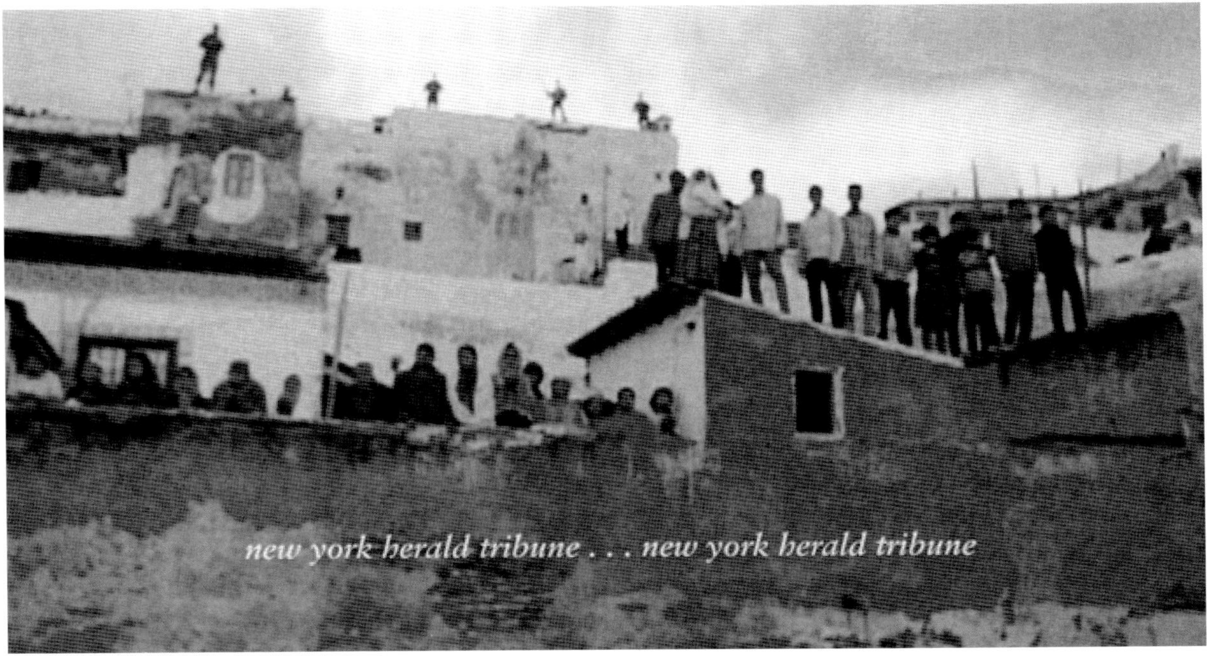
new york herald tribune . . . new york herald tribune

dead editorials, living obituaries

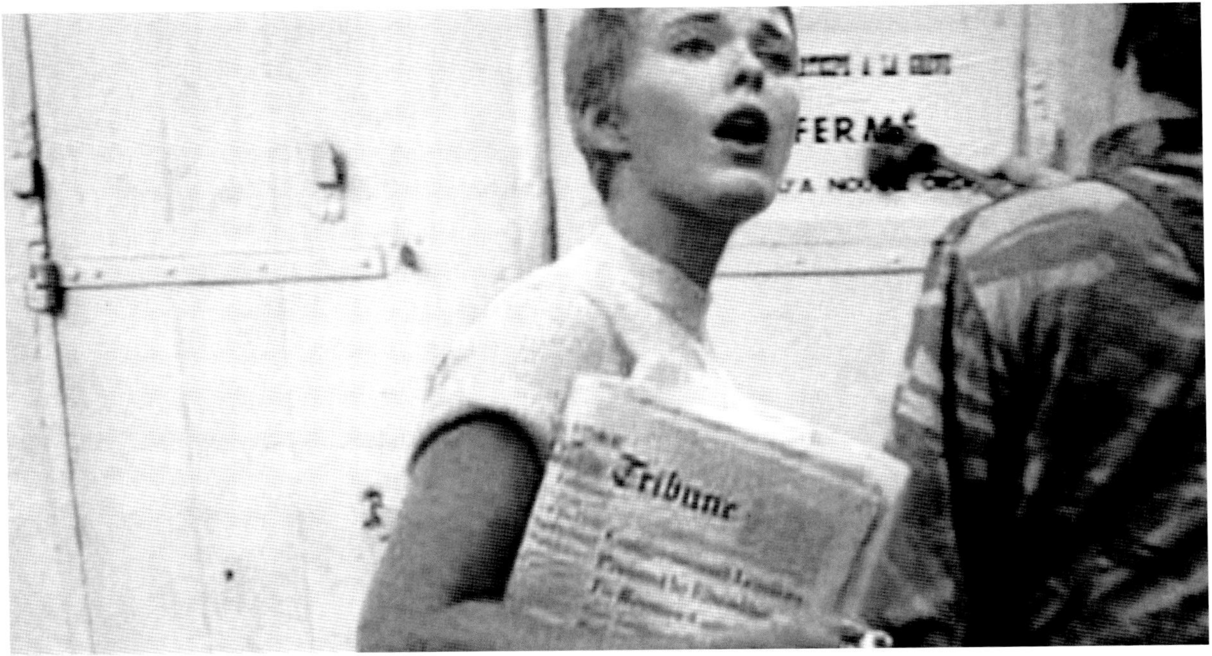
FERMÉ
Tribune

no body count in the real estate section

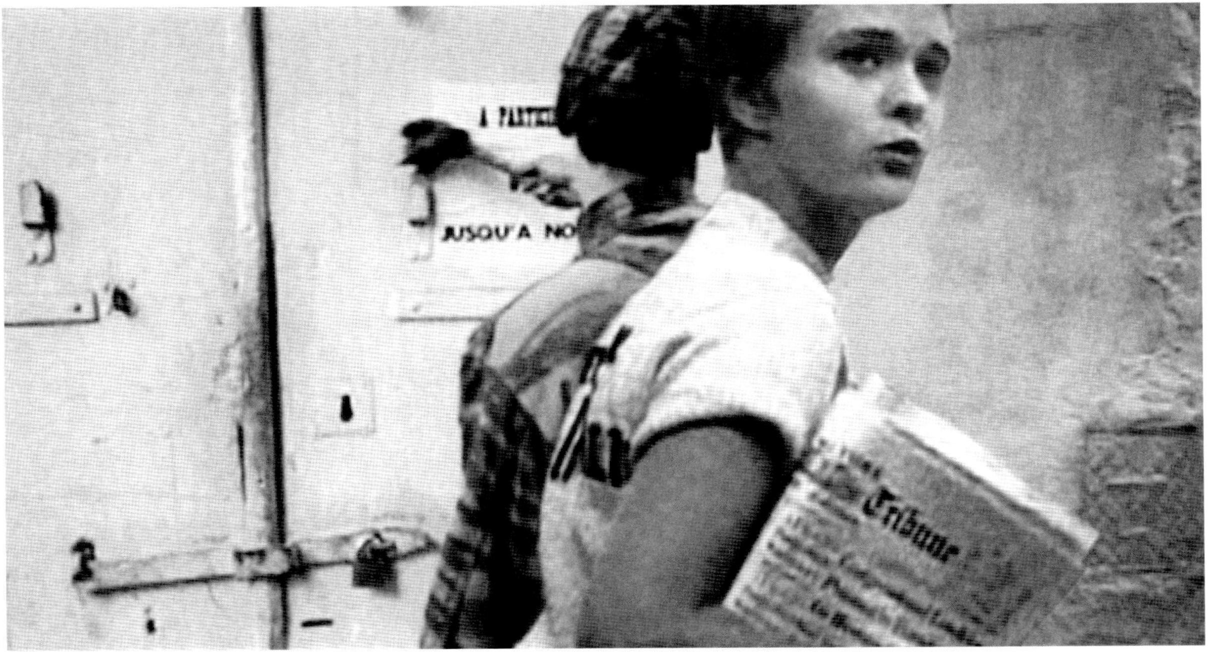
JUSQU'A
Tribune

circulating the news or circulating around it

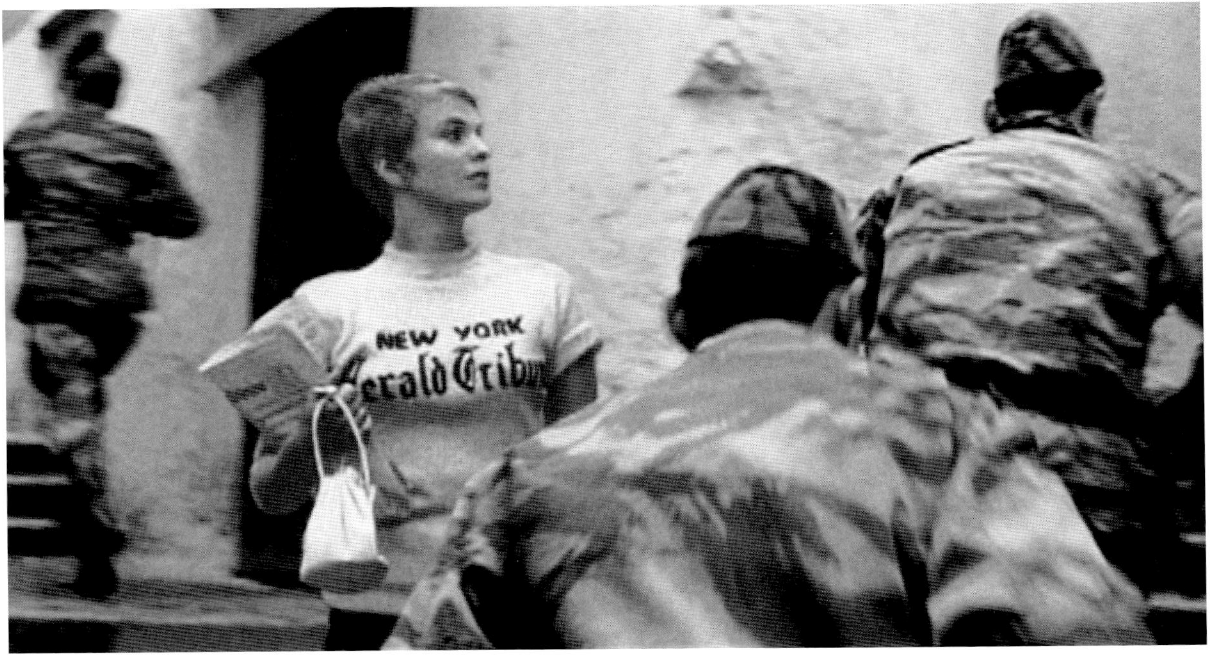
NEW YORK

events and the news of events struggling over territory

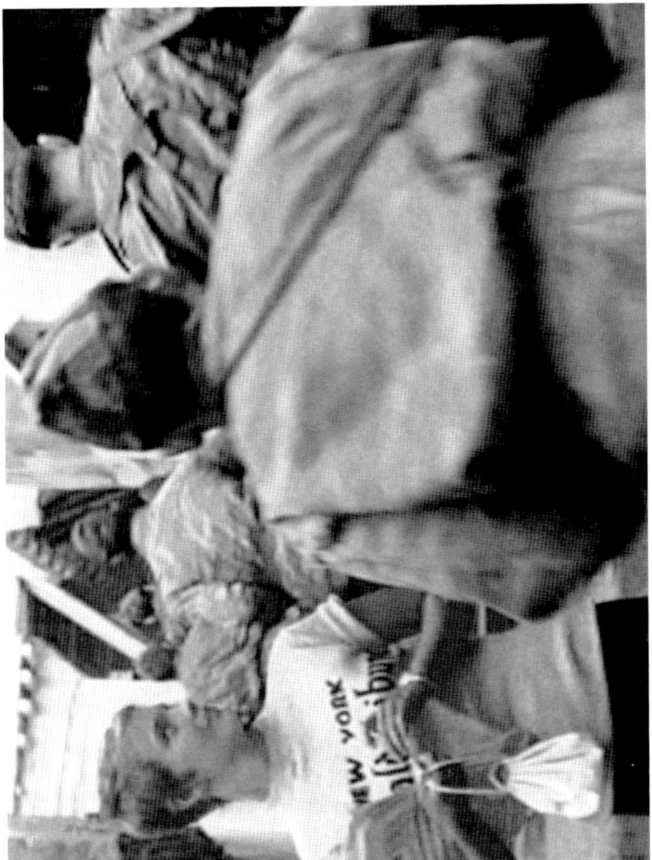

the flowering of signs

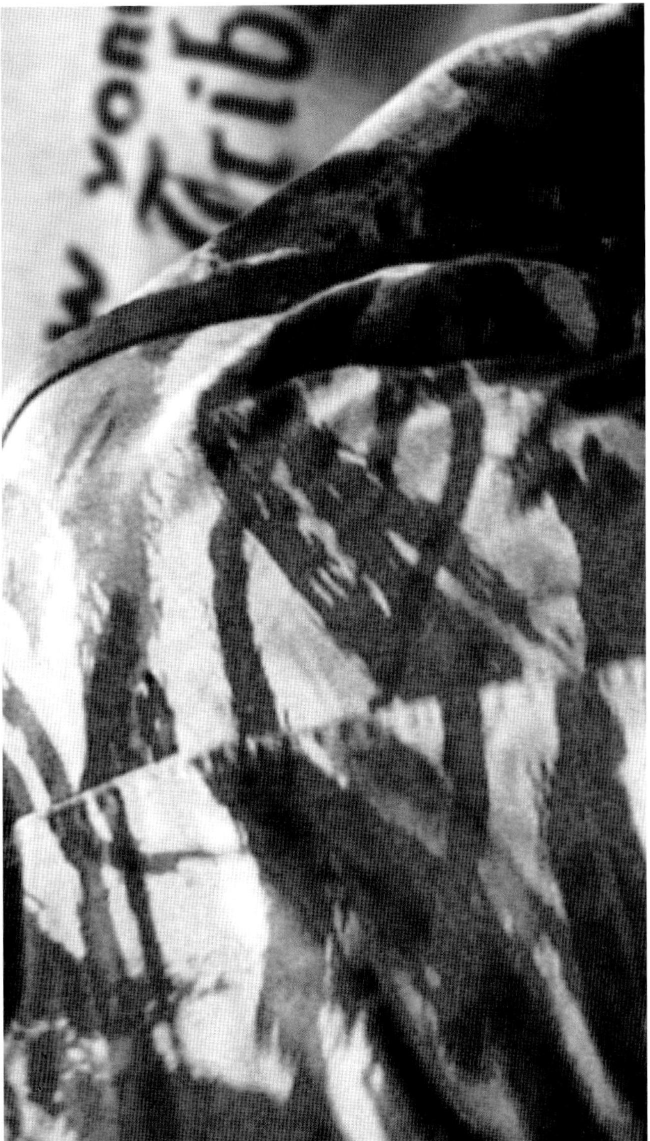

the turning away in turning around and around

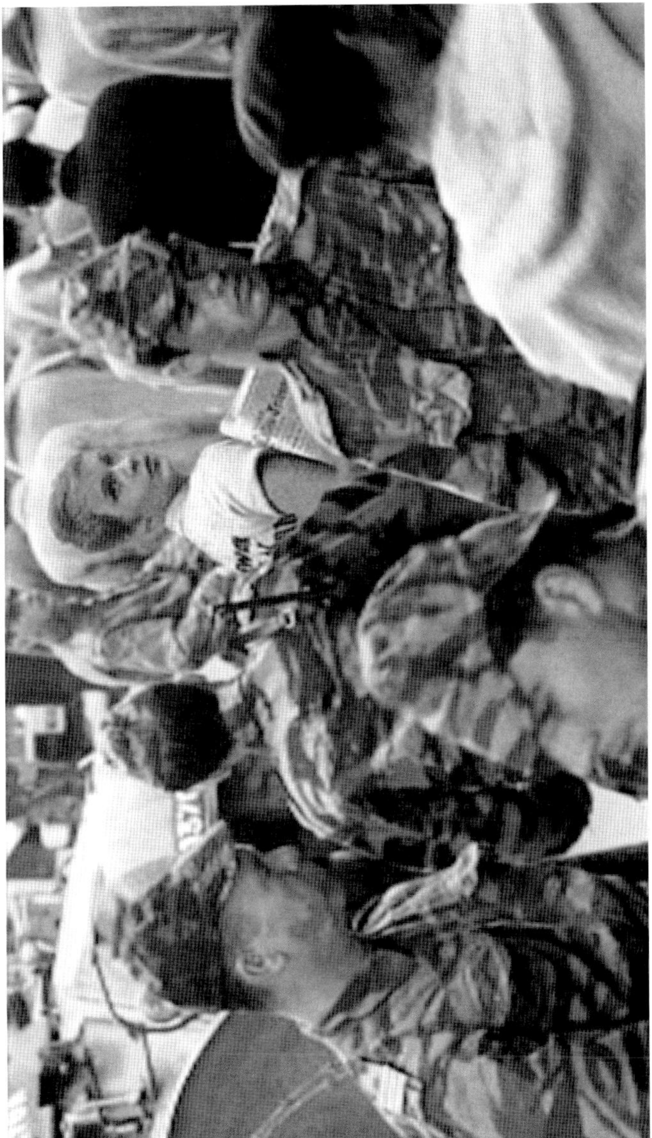

surrendering to events—the slope of the cinema's floor

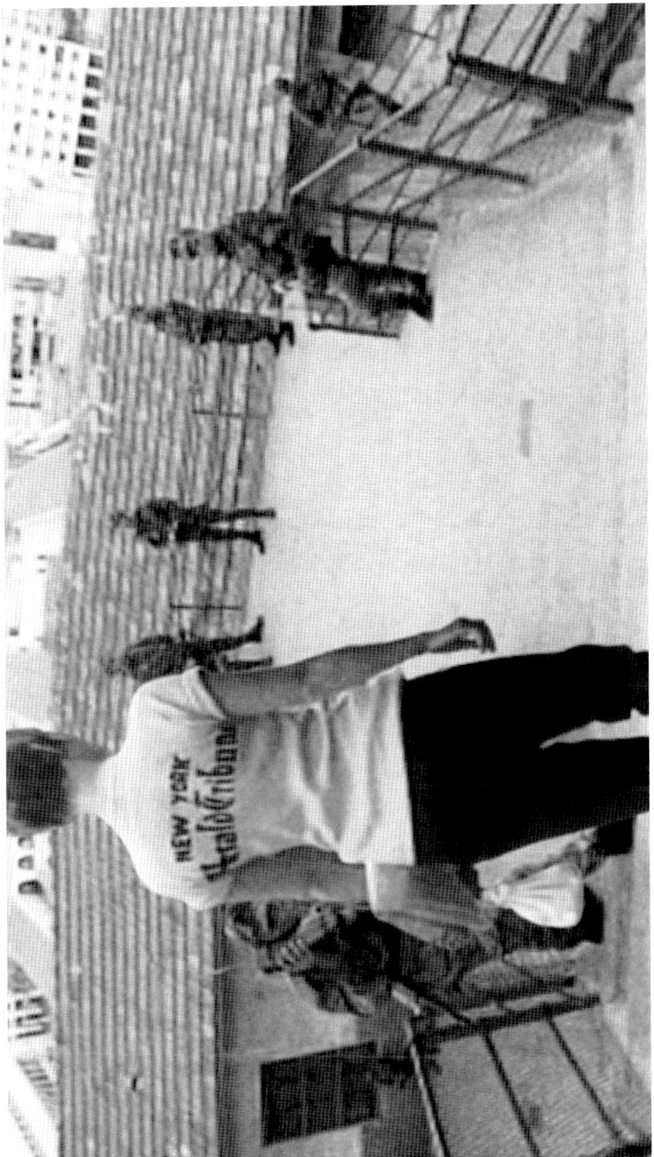
NEW YORK
Herald Tribune

the fool knows her stage is borrowed

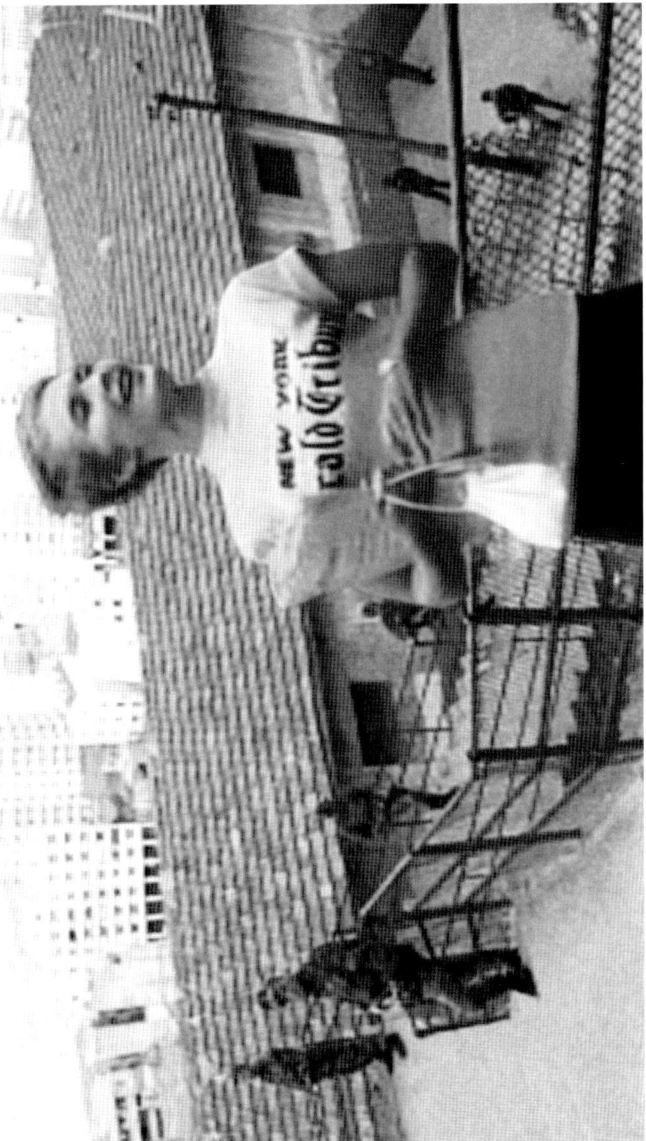
NEW YORK

the condition of entering the cinema from the rear

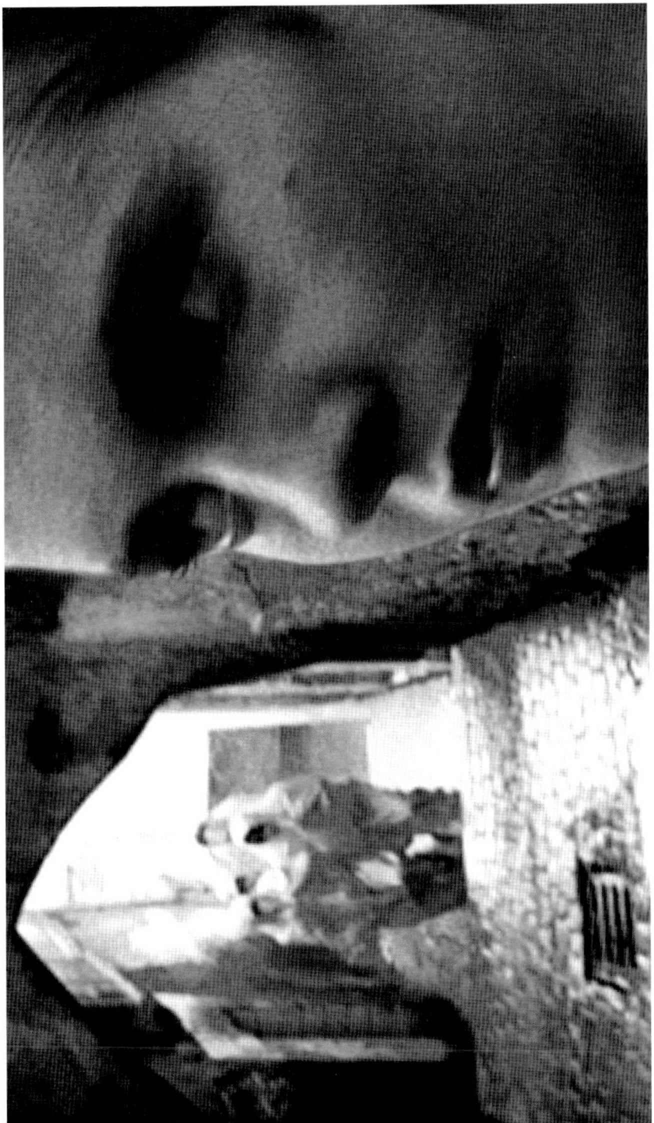

sleeper cell awakening in a dream

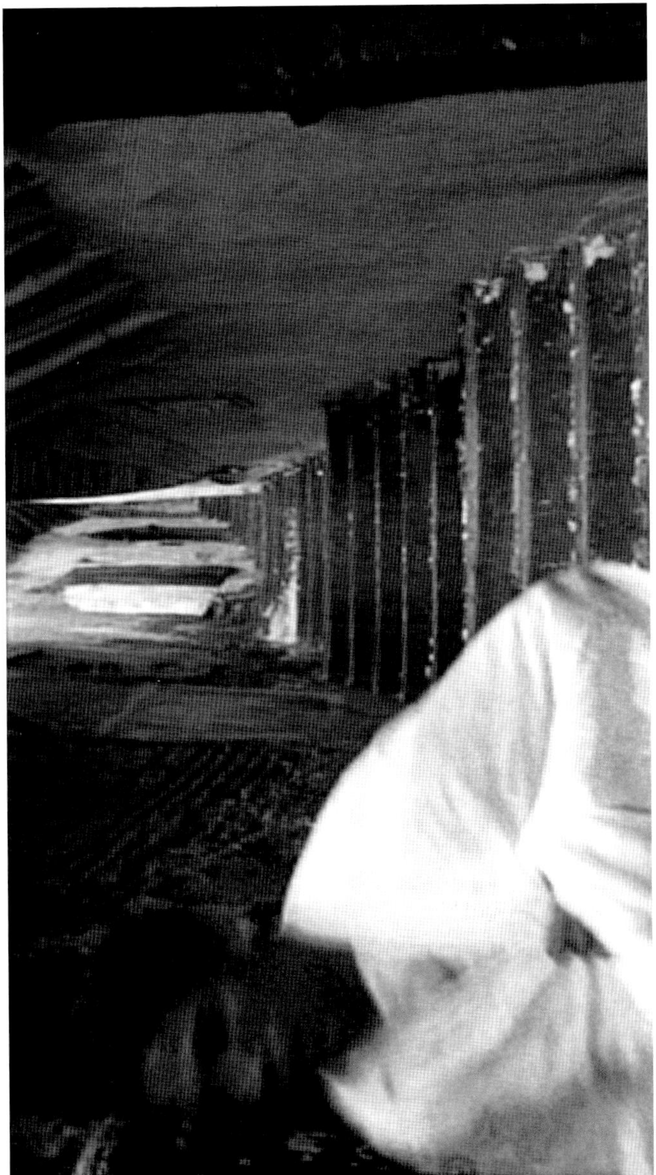

missteps neither real nor fiction

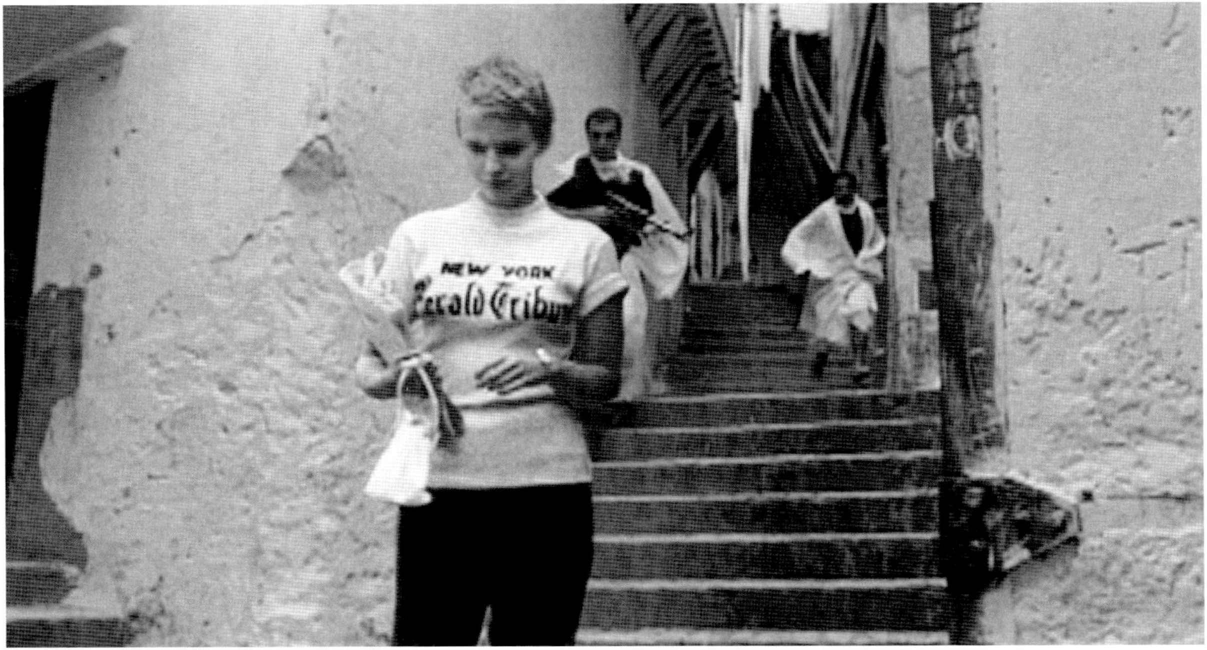
NEW YORK

crude costumes at the end of the parade

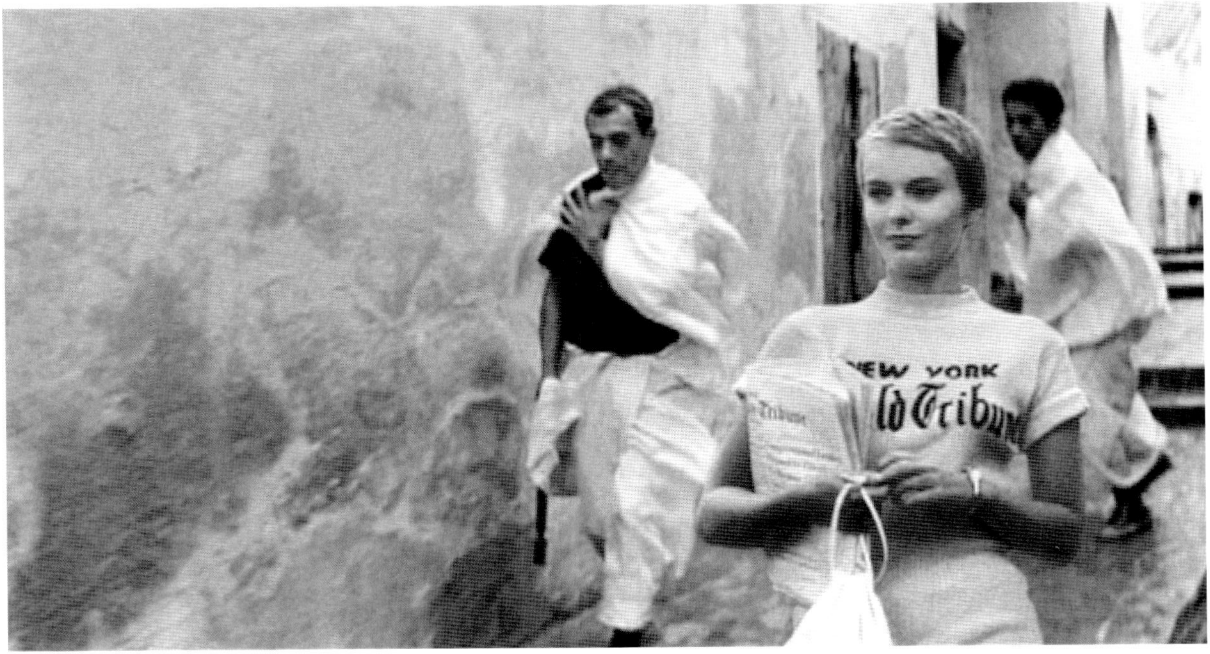
EW YORK

the old order in profile, the three-quarter view of now

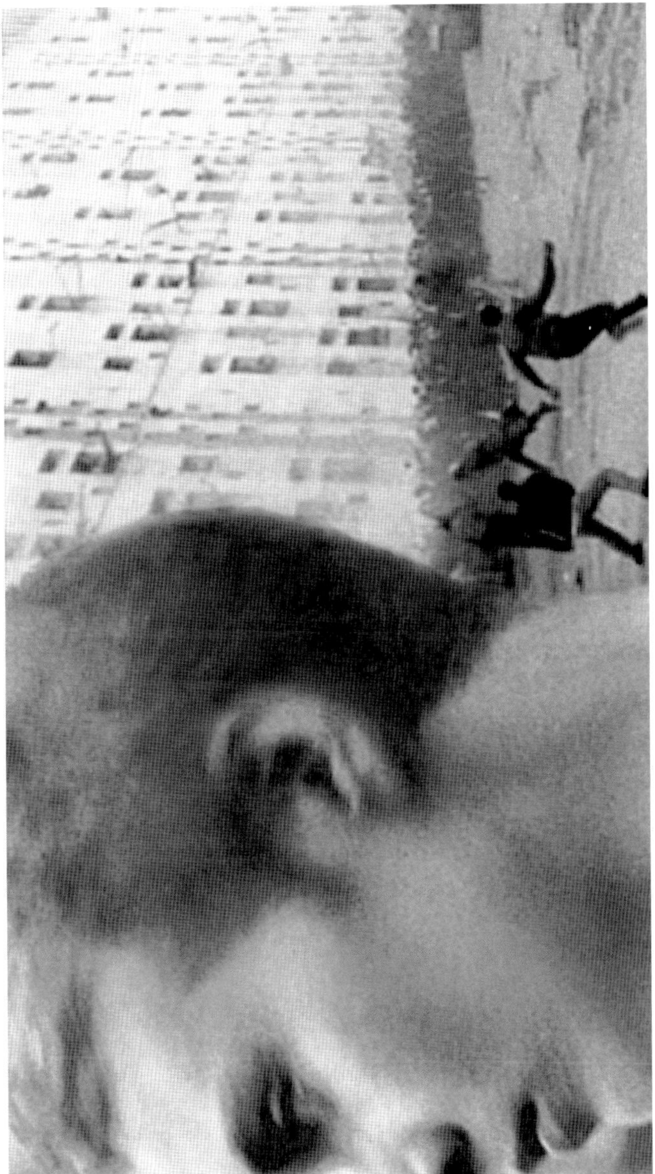

innocence of the nape when the face has been found guilty

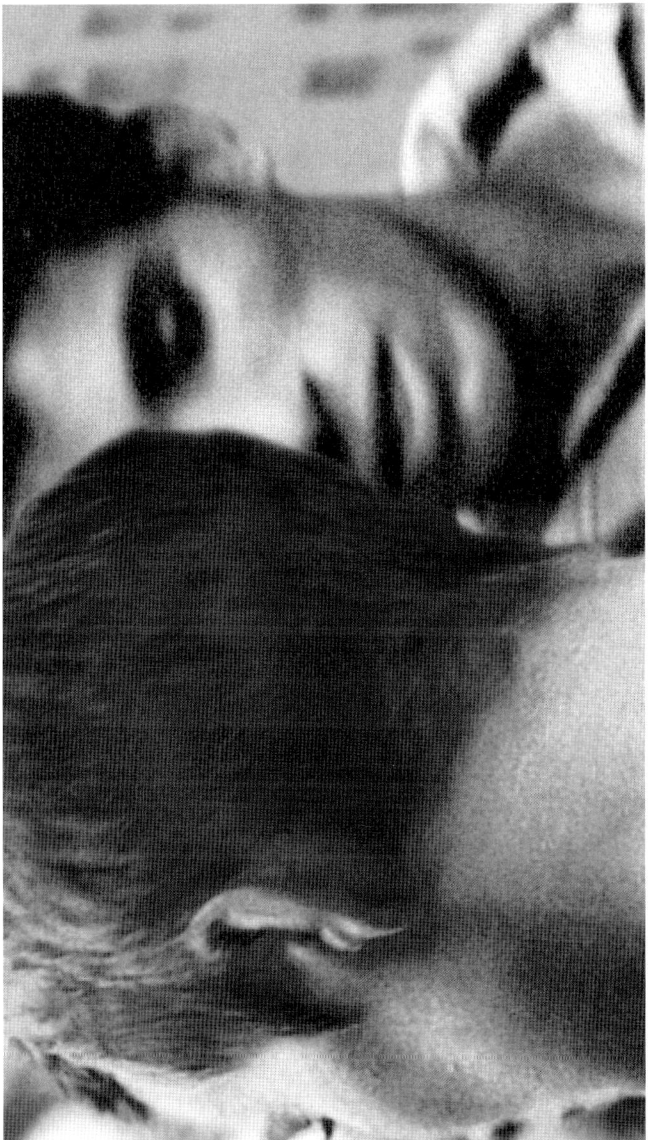

more alone in stop frame

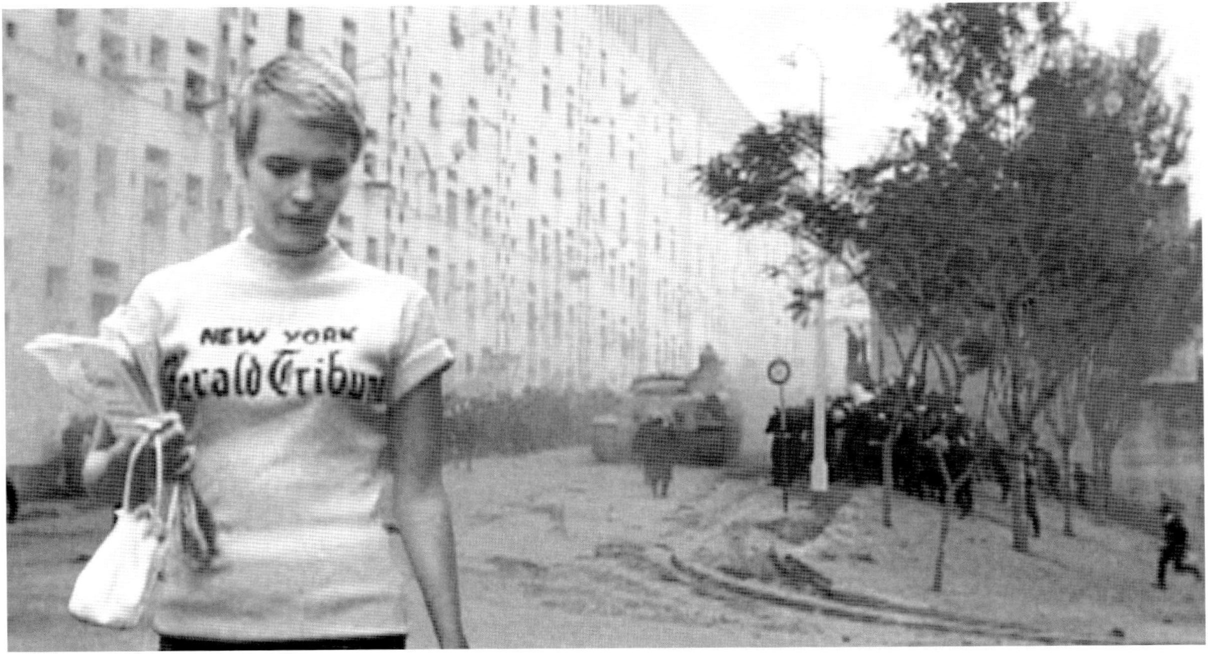
NEW YORK

no longer in time but surrounded by time

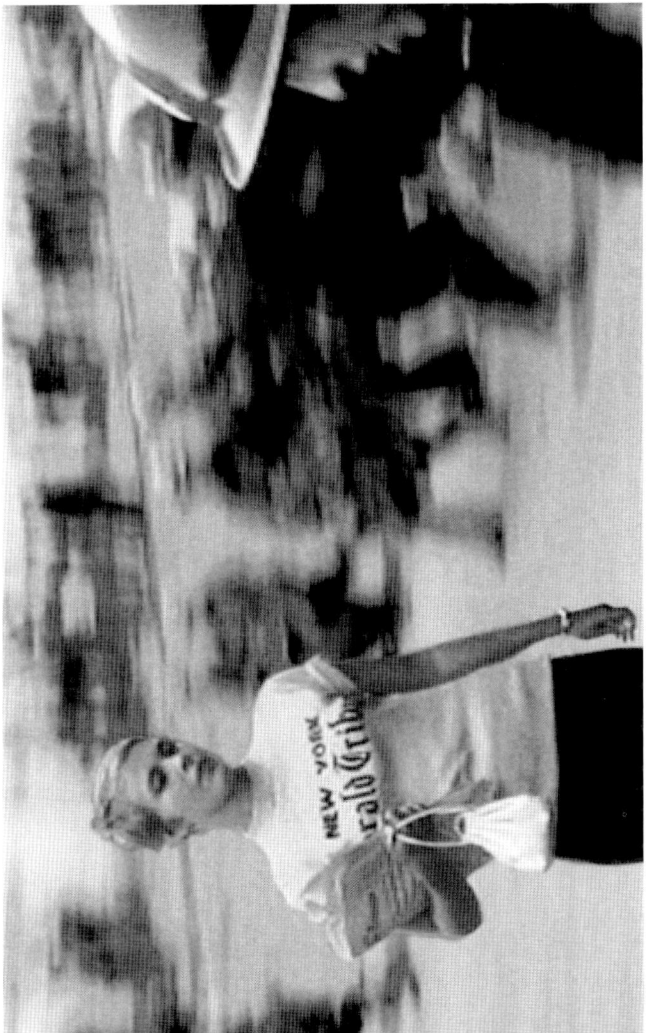
NEW YORK

advancing toward zero

more panicked in the wrong film

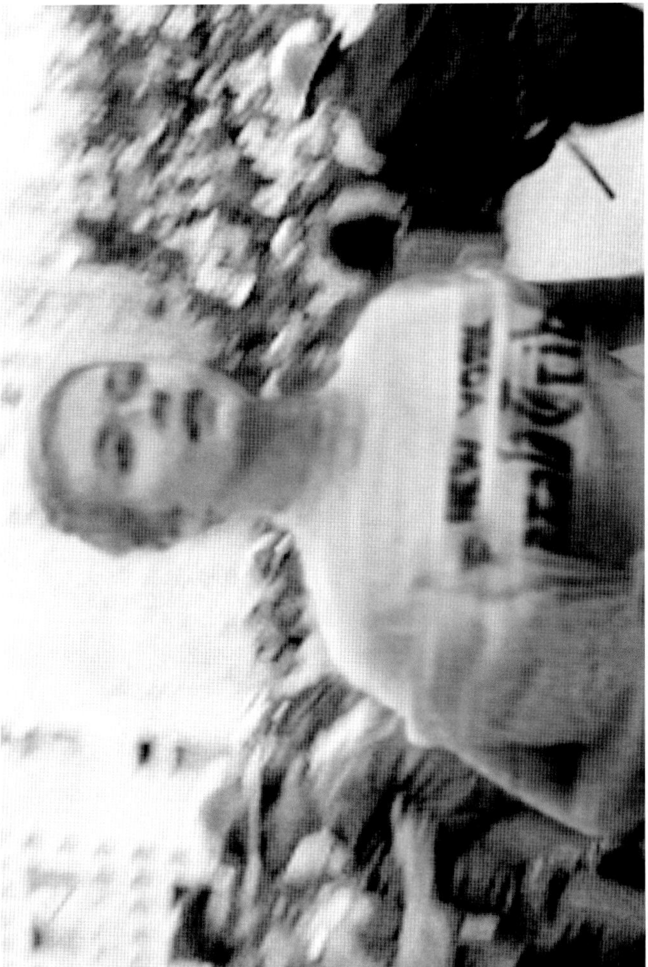

if you can’t read the signs they belong to the enemy

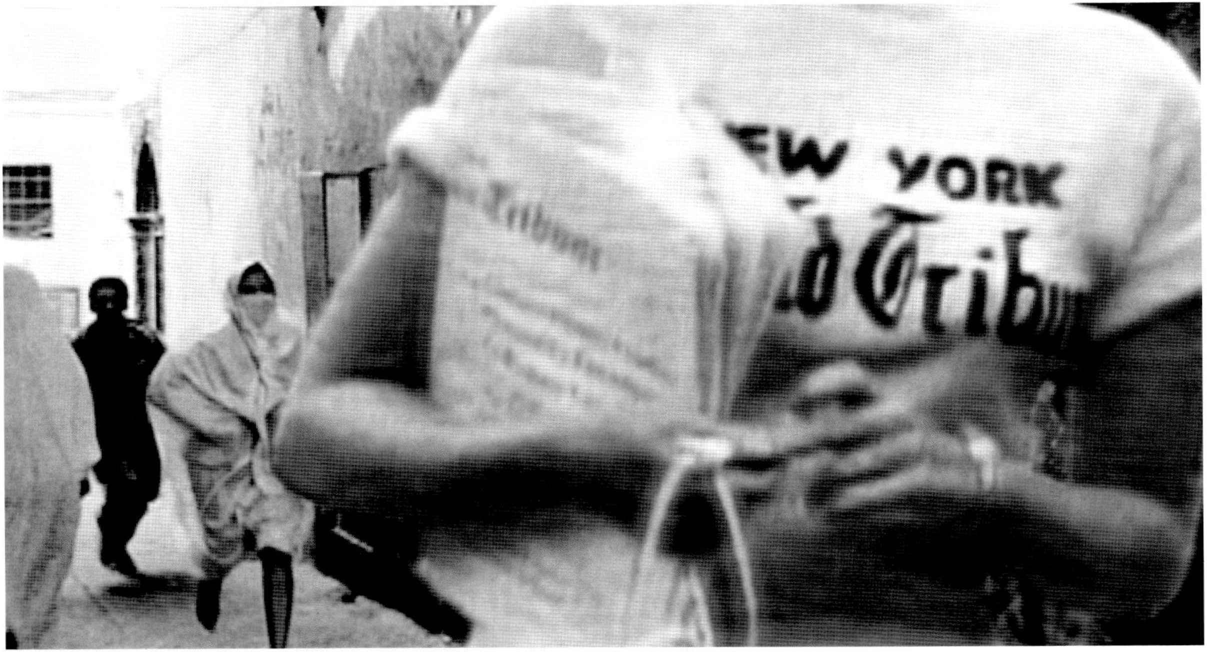
EW YORK

dead or alive or wanted

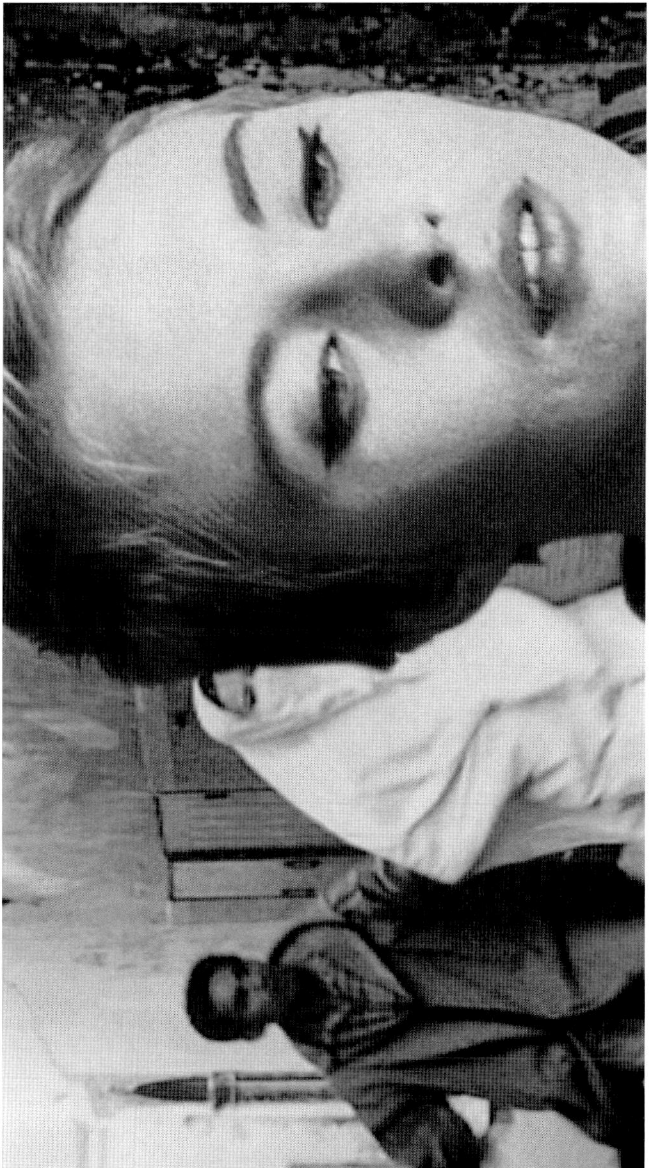

the solidarity of masquerades

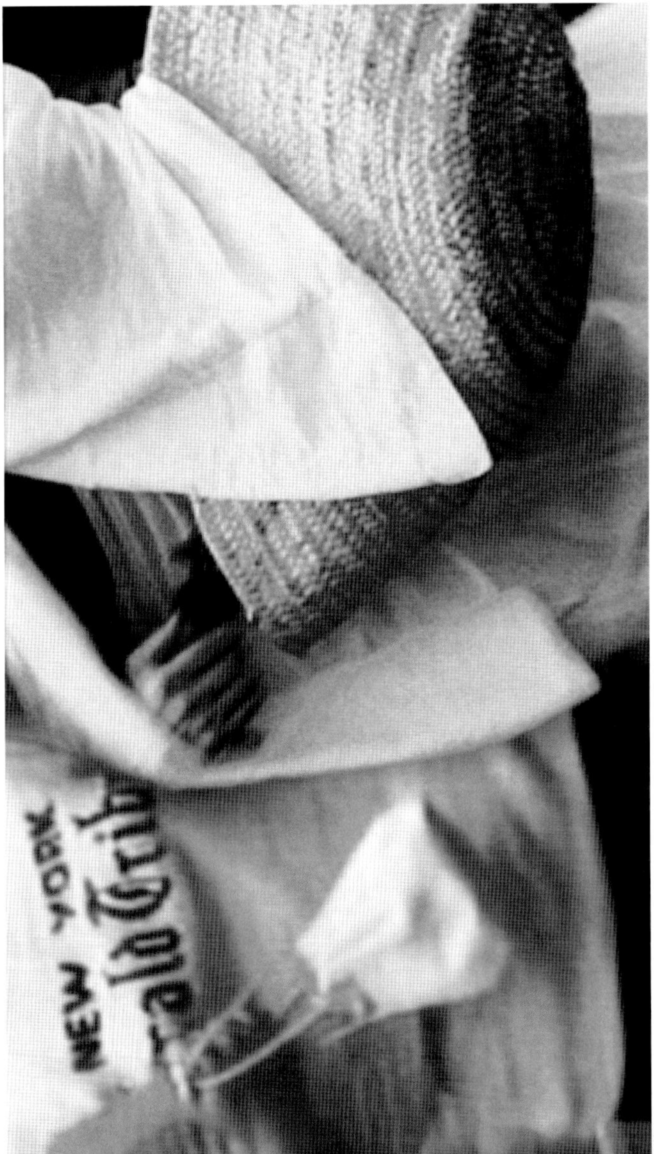
NEW YORK

the news in the news hawker's eyes

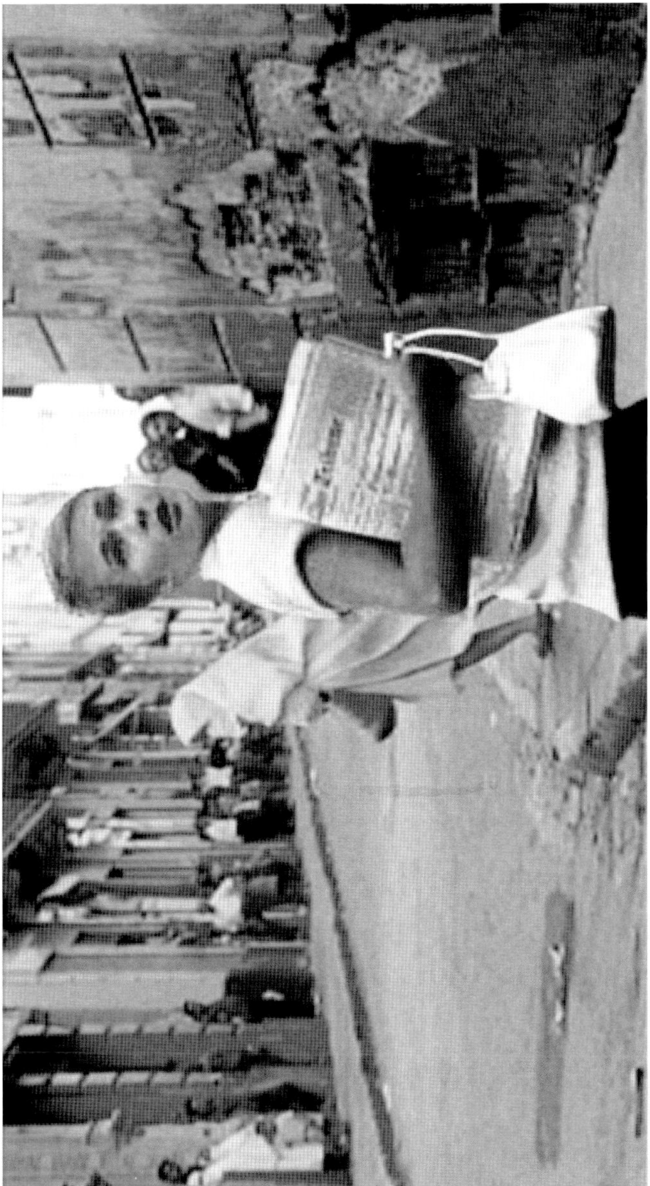

overheard: they can see our women, we can't see theirs

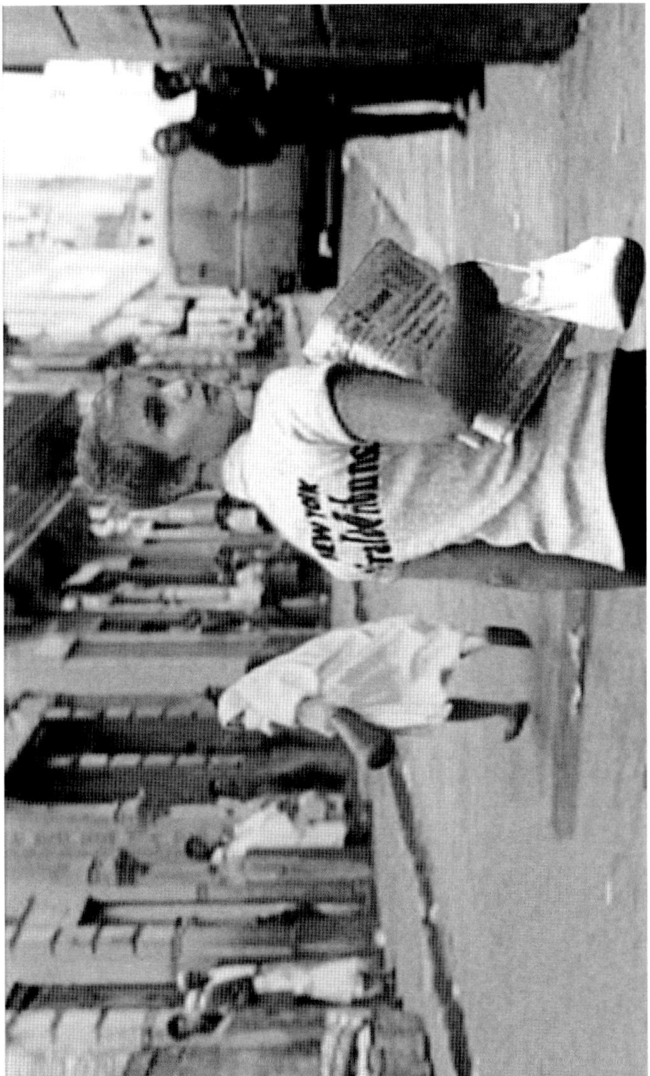

the sandwich board as the perfect combination of rage and modesty—invented by Zola

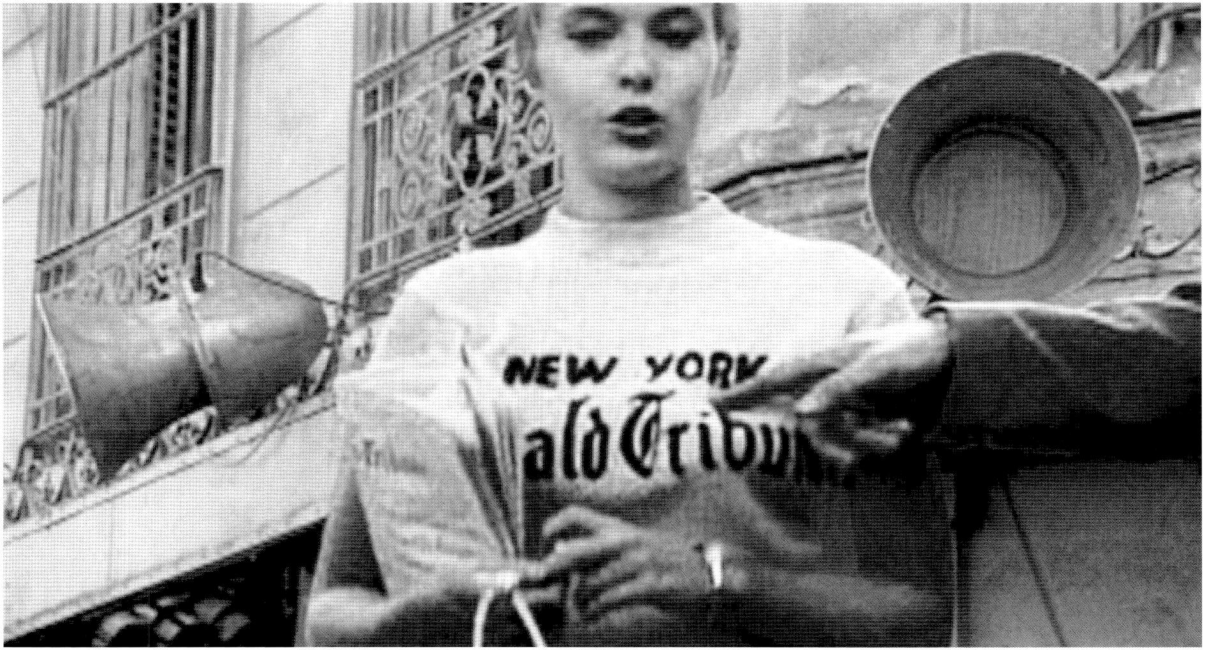
NEW YORK

private moments or public warnings

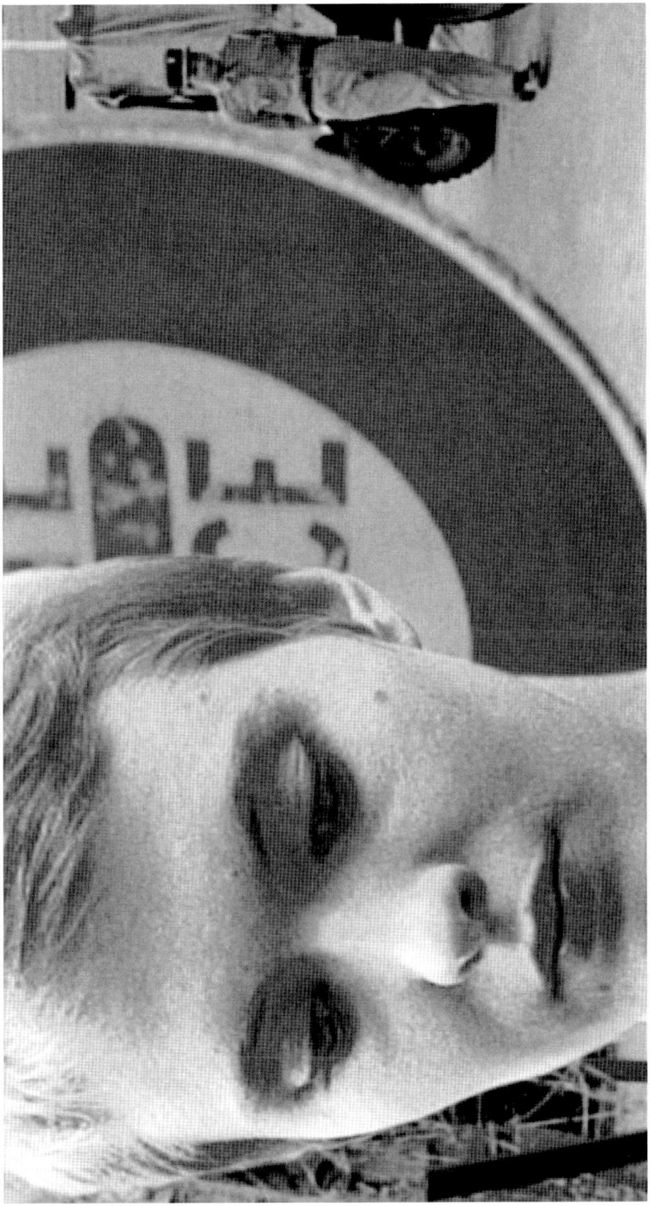

borders within borders, riddles without a sphinx

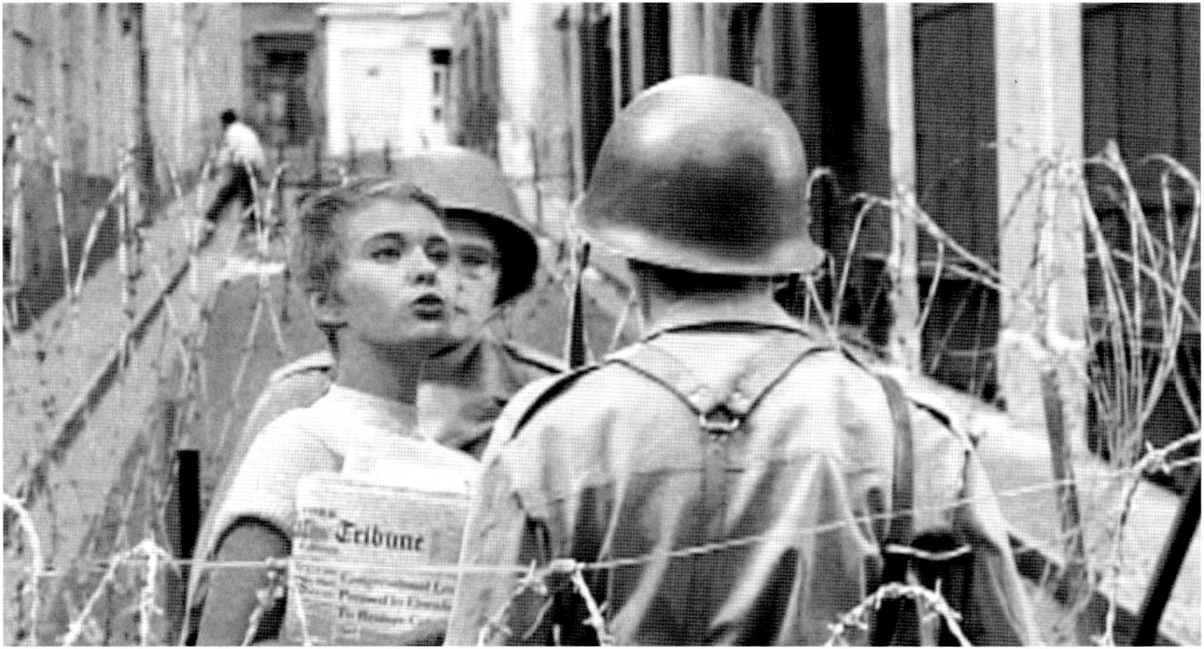
Tribune

leaving to make an image of leaving

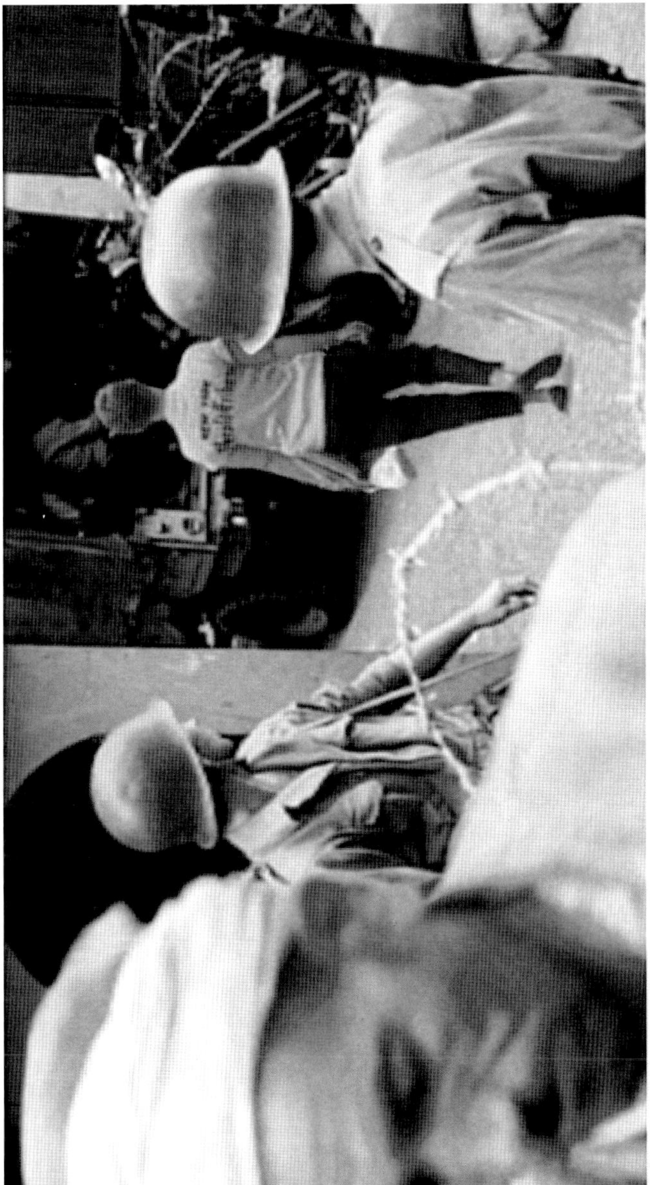

the foot left behind the other—satisfied

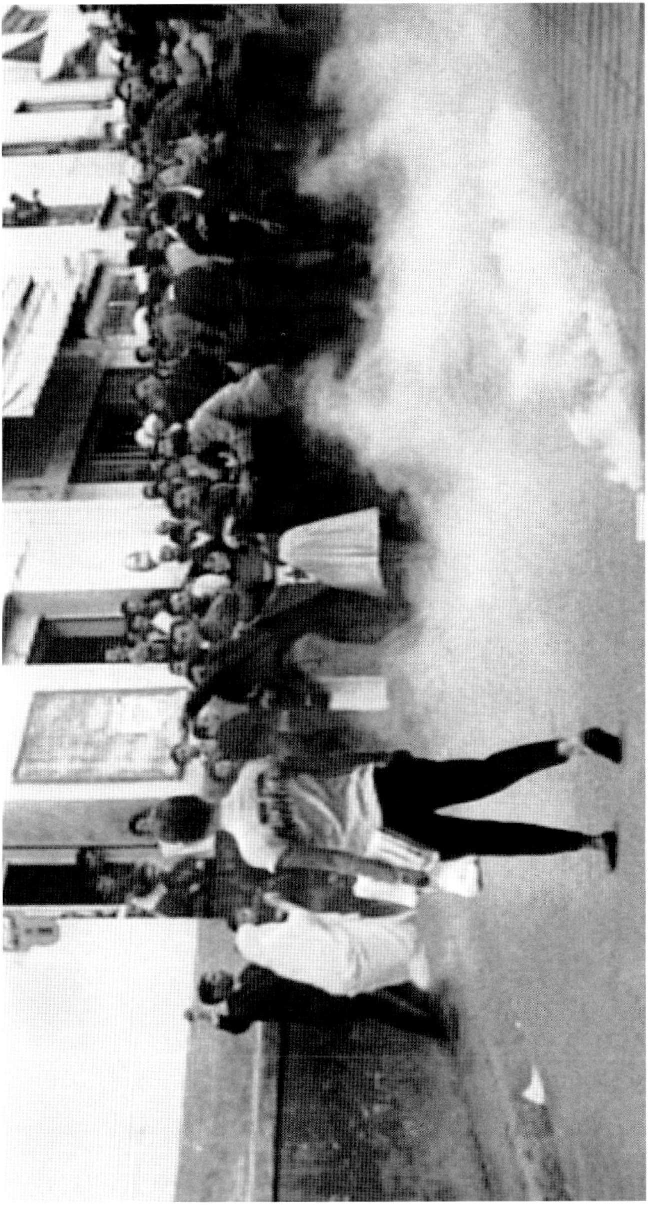

out of step

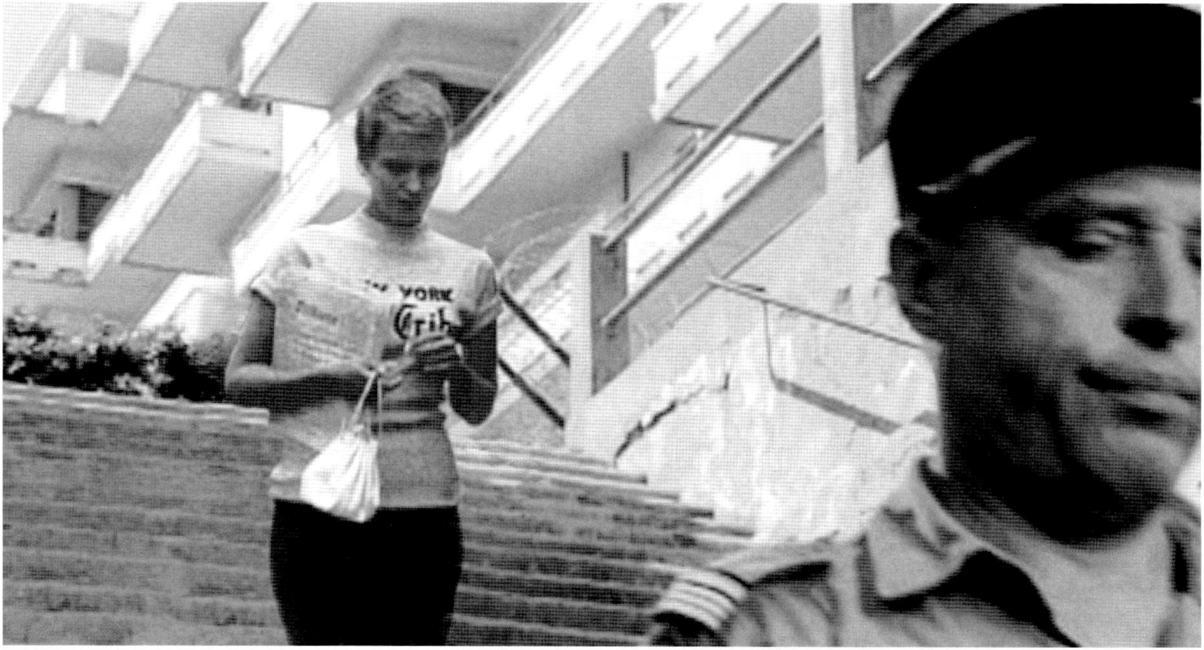
YORK

closing the distance

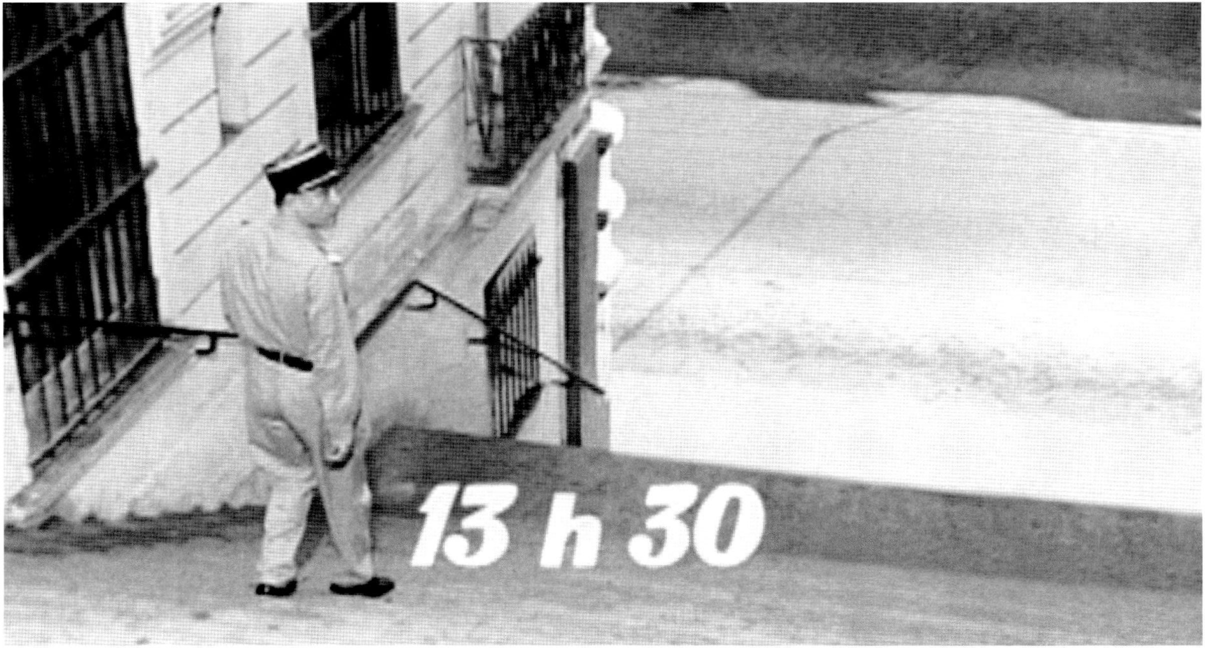
13 h 30

violence redeems itself in a series of small tests

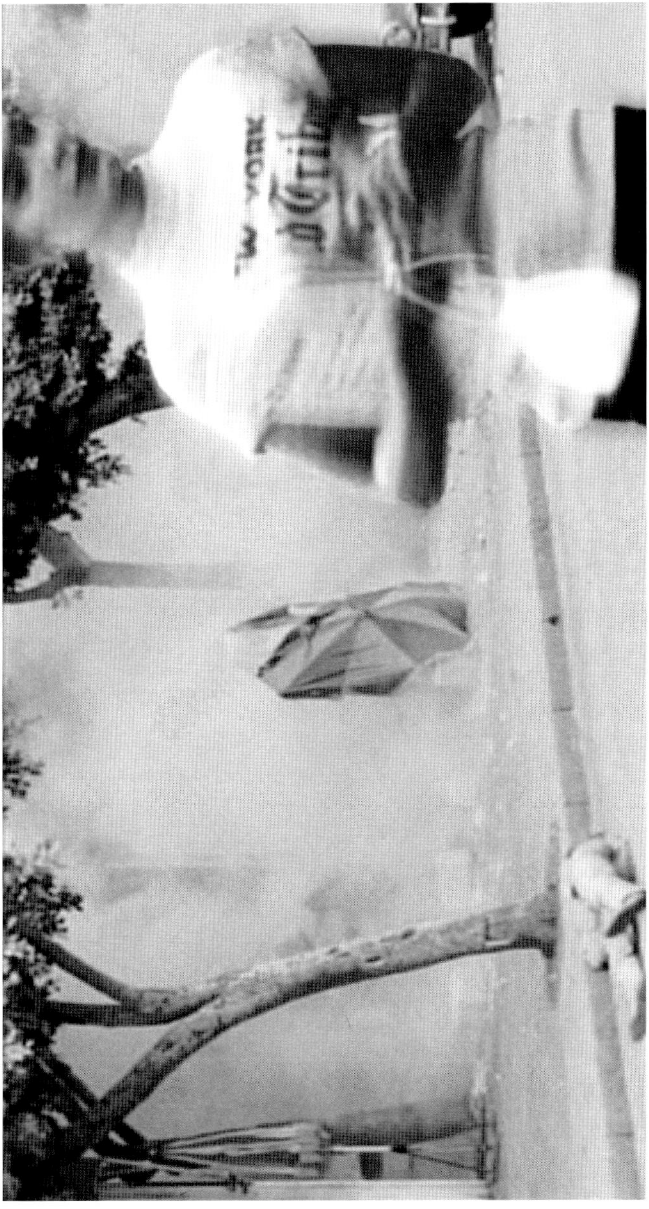

the dead are counted but not the images of the dead

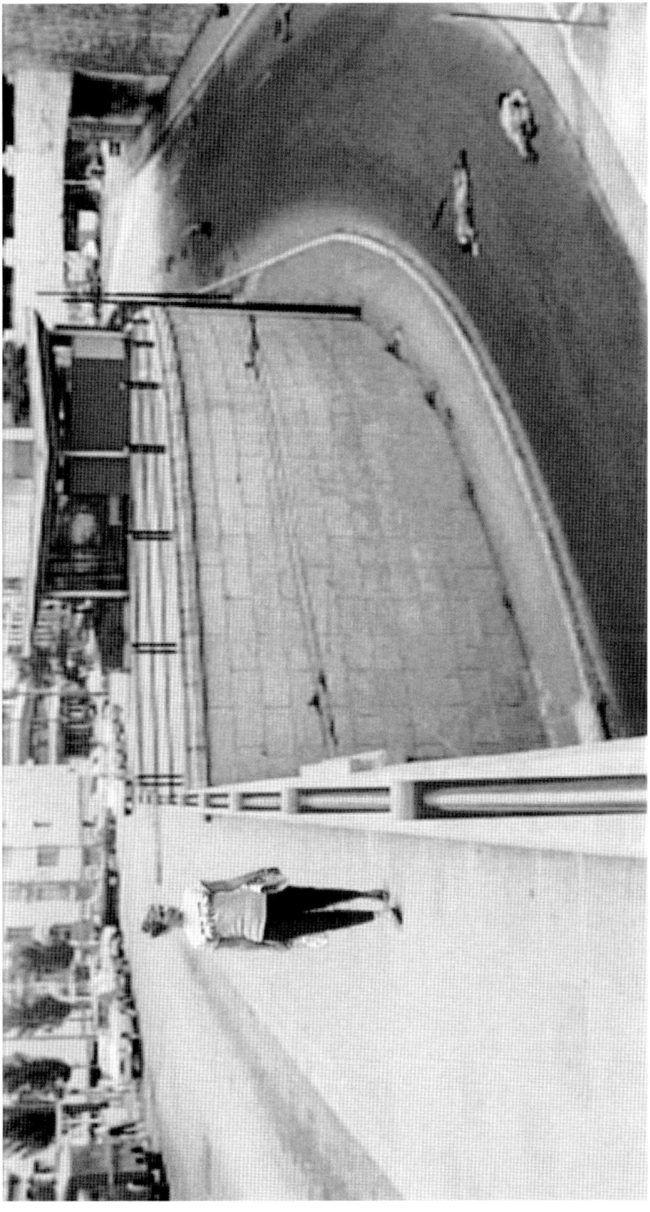

fast forward to Mecca

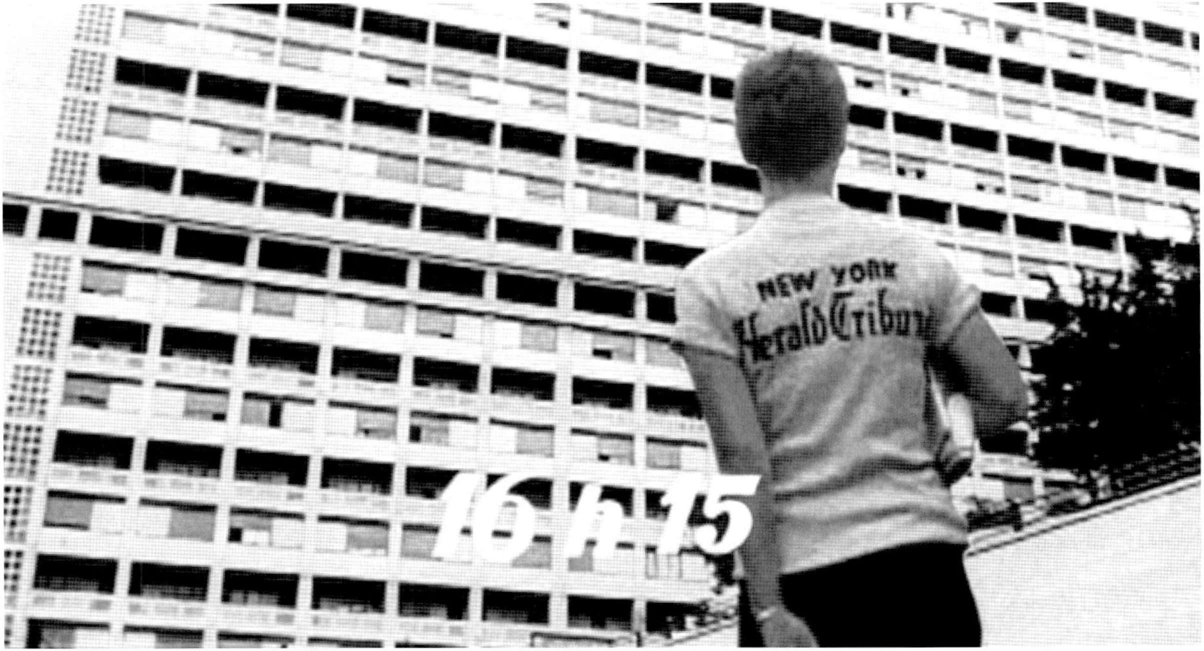
NEW YORK
16 h 15

new intimacies in revolution

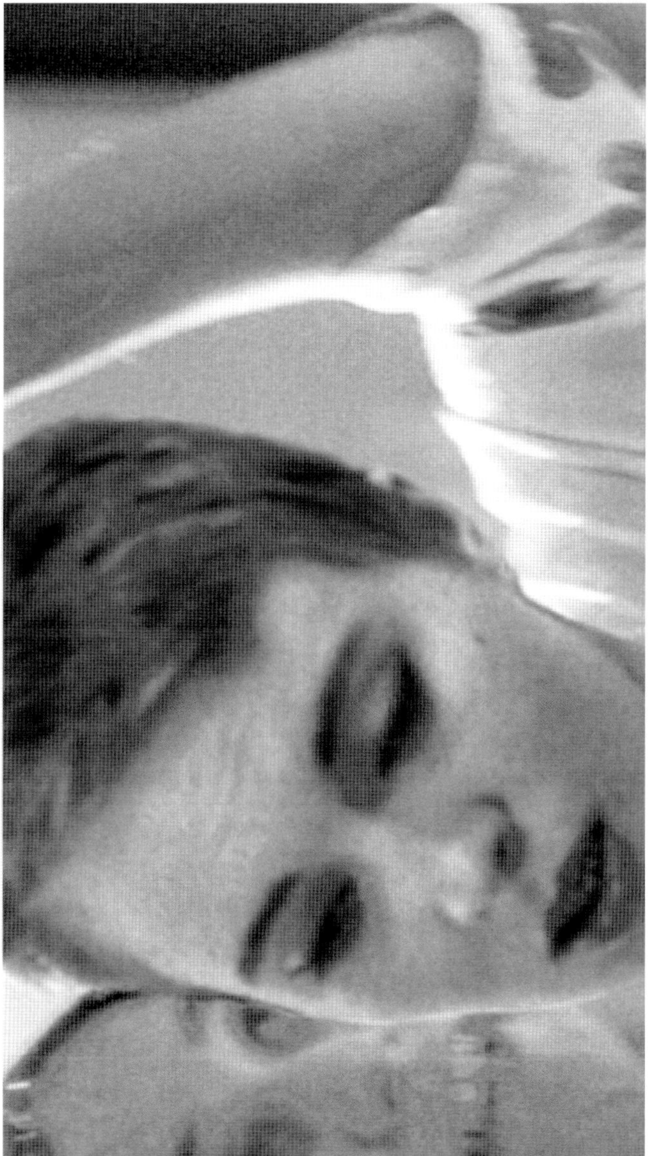

fear of the hooker’s total knowledge

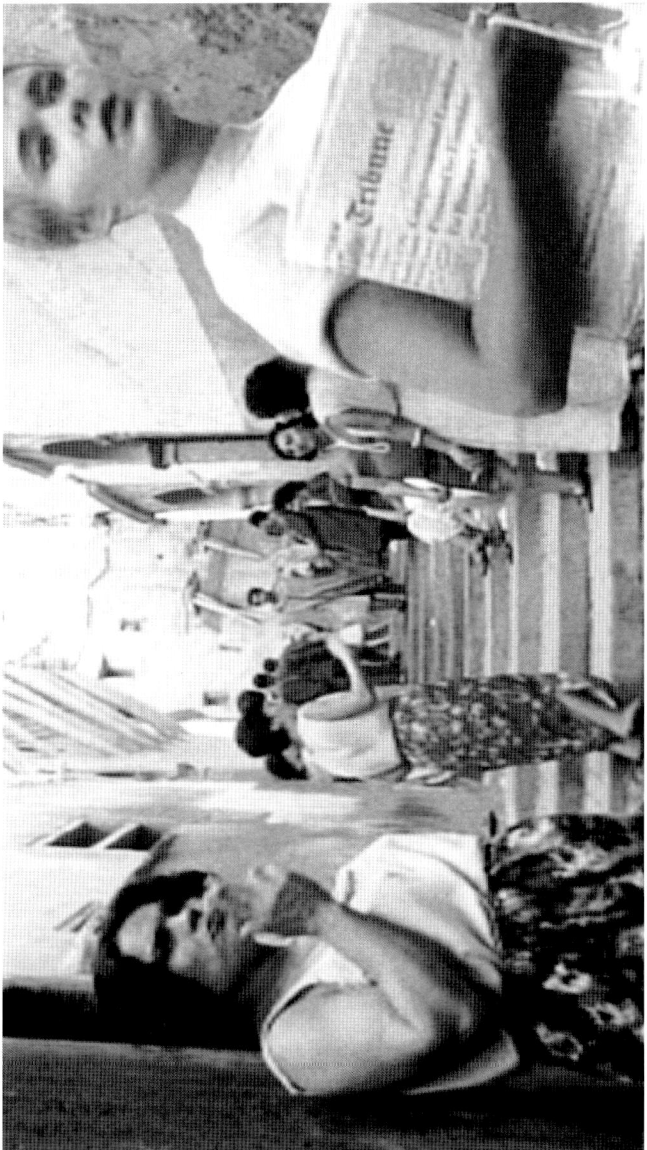
Tribune

smoke

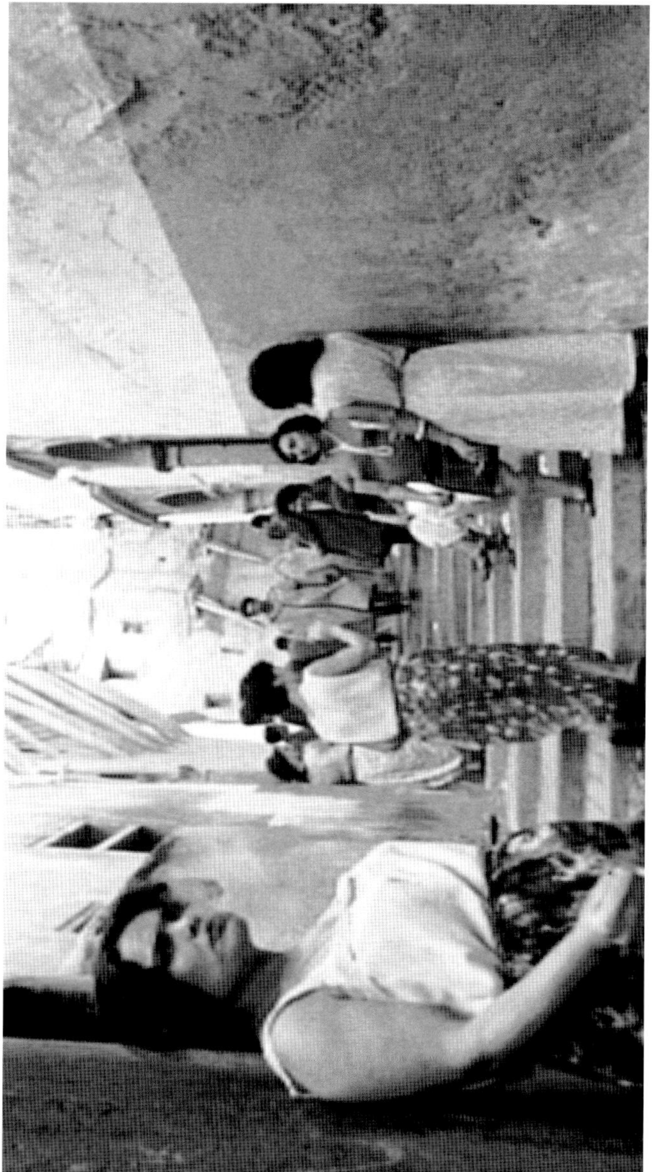

default to Jean Seberg—chameleon daydreaming in her own color

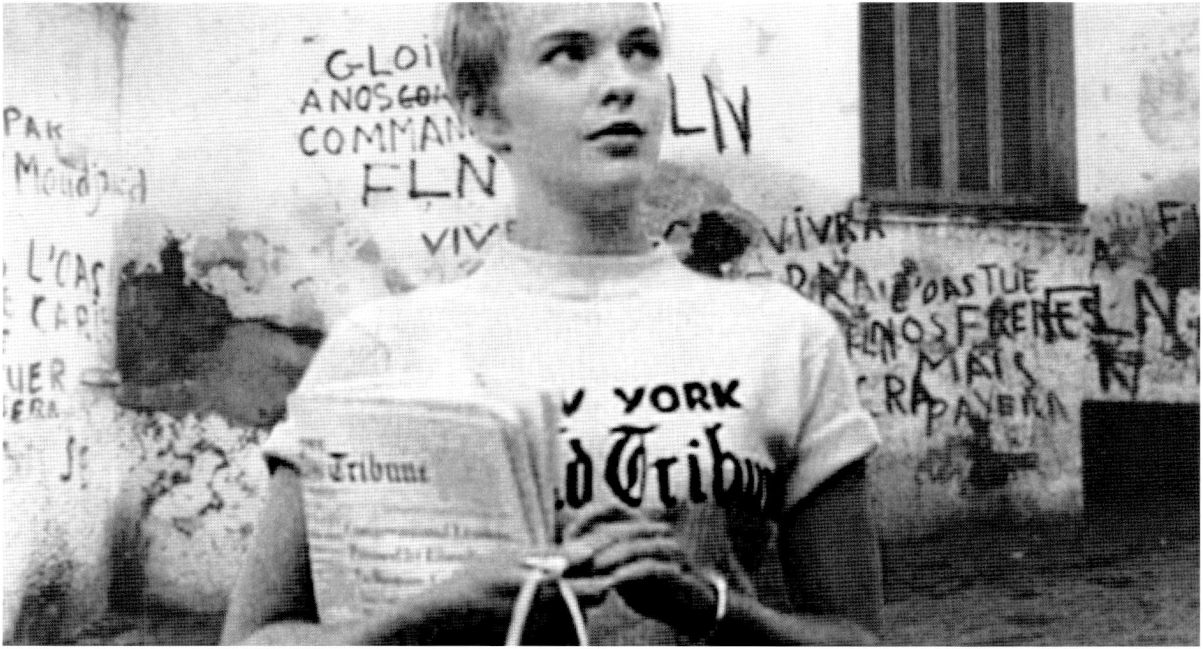

GLOI
ANOS
COMMAN
FLN
VIVRA
Y YORK
Tribune

not on the Champs-Élysées

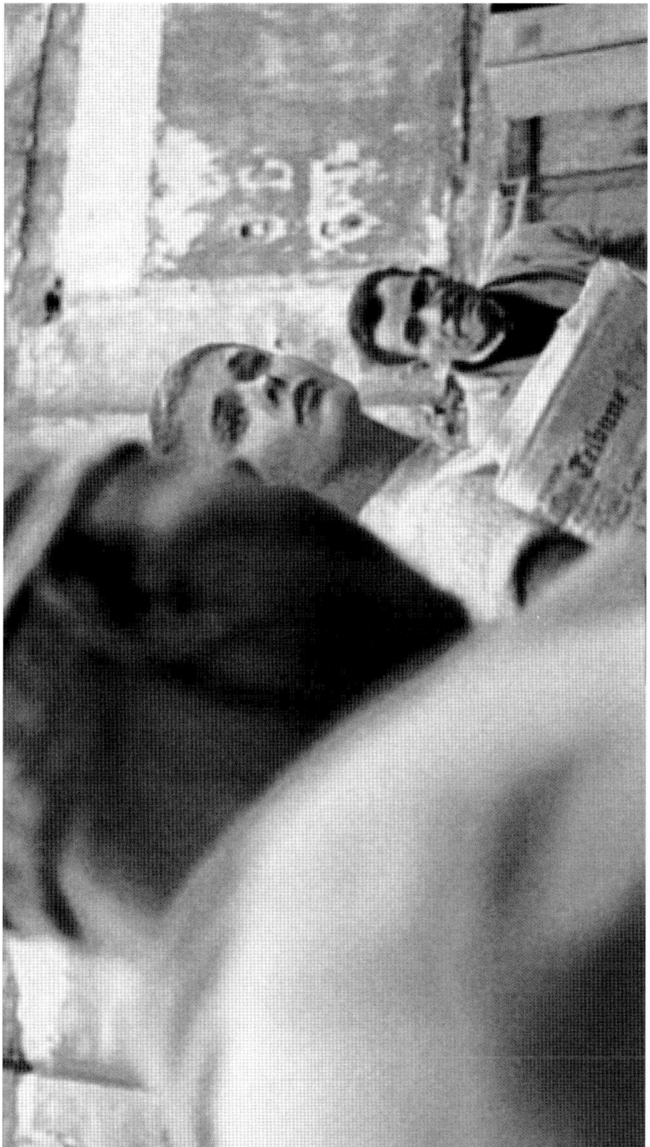

curtain call to see all the characters touching

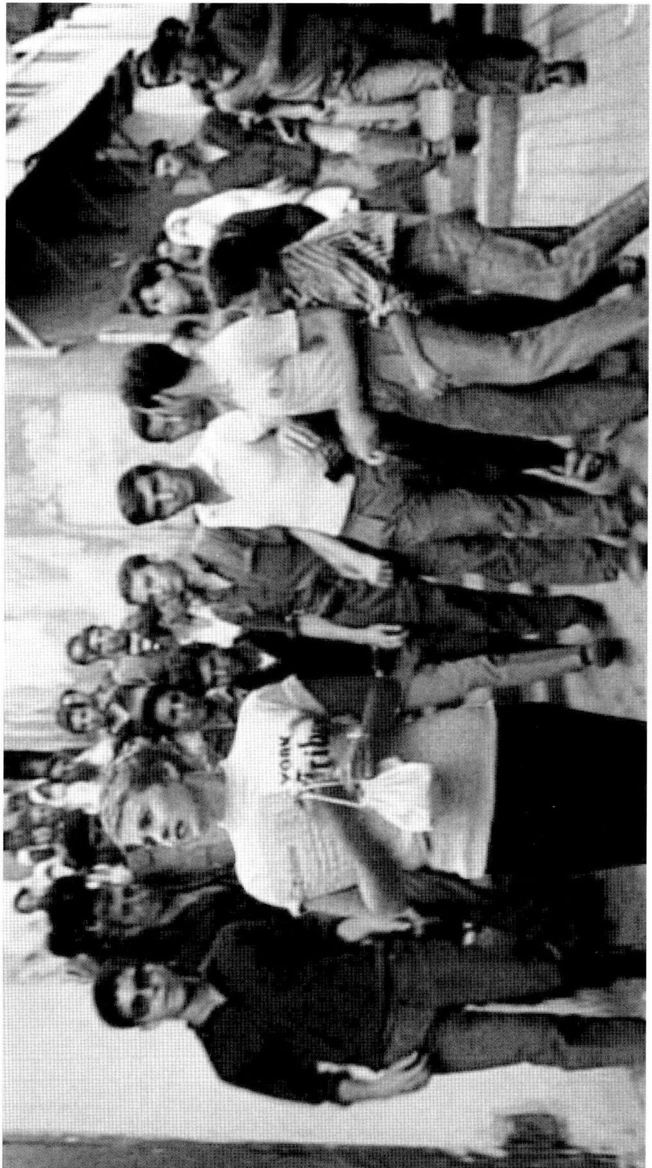

Jean Seberg, born and raised in Marshalltown, Iowa, was only seventeen in 1955 when she was chosen from thousands of hopeful young actresses by director Otto Preminger to star as Joan of Arc in his film of George Bernard Shaw's *Saint Joan*. In Seberg's next film, *Bonjour Tristesse*, also directed by Preminger, her role as a spoiled pixyish adolescent vacationing with her playboy father on the French Riviera inspired a young Godard to cast her opposite Belmondo in *Breathless*, which would become a New Wave sensation. In total Seberg made thirty-four films, which also included *The Mouse That Roared*, *Lilith*, *Paint Your Wagon*, and *Airport*. In the late 60s and early 70s, Seberg's political empathy and sexual relationship with Hakim Jamal, a charismatic player in the Black Power movement, as well as her financial support of the Black Panther Party led the FBI to monitor her activities and smear her reputation in the media. She never fully recovered from the scandal and over the next several years became increasingly dependent on alcohol and prescription drugs. On September 9, 1979, Jean Seberg was found dead in her parked car in a Paris suburb. The autopsy revealed she had overdosed on barbiturates and alcohol. After a lengthy investigation her death was ruled a suicide by the Paris police.

Dennis Adams is internationally recognized for his urban interventions and museum installations that reveal historical and political undercurrents in public space and architecture. Over the last two decades he has produced more than fifty projects worldwide in cities from Antwerp to Zagreb. His work has been the subject of numerous one-person exhibitions in museums and galleries throughout North America and Europe, and is included in major public collections both here and abroad, including the Museum of Contemporary Art, Chicago; Museum of Modern Art, New York; Walker Art Center, Minneapolis; Whitney Museum of American Art, New York; Fonds National d'Art Contemporain, Paris; Museum van Hedendaagse Kunst, Antwerp; the Städtische Galerie im Lenbachhaus, Munich; and the Fotomuseum Winterthur, Zurich.

Adams has taught at numerous institutions including Parsons School of Design, New York; École Nationale Supérieure des Beaux-Arts, Paris; Rijksakademie van Beeldende Kunsten, Amsterdam; and the Akademie der Bildenden Künste, Munich. From 1997 to 2001 he was Director of the Visual Arts Program and Professor in the School of Architecture at MIT. He is currently a Professor in the School of Art at the Cooper Union in New York.